ANTICIPATE THE COMING RESERVOIR

BOOKS BY JOHN HOPPENTHALER

Lives of Water
Anticipate the Coming Reservoir

ANTICIPATE THE COMING RESERVOIR

POEMS BY JOHN HOPPENTHALER

CARNEGIE MELLON UNIVERSITY PRESS
PITTSBURGH 2008

Grateful acknowledgment is made to editors of the following publications in which many of these poems first appeared:

ABZ: "Sex in Public Places"; *Alehouse:* "Treehouse"; *Barrow Street:* "Arts & Crafts"; *Blueline:* "A Fall Poem," "North on the Palisades Parkway"; *Carnegie Mellon Poetry Journal:* "Ice Jesus," "Silver Wings"; *Cave Wall:* "Something is Out There," "Key West," "Odd Man Out," "Oh, Danny Boy"; *Chance of a Ghost,* Helicon Nine Editions, 2005: "Ashokan: A Catskill Story"; *Chautauqua Literary Journal:* "A Jar of Rain"; *The Dirty Napkin:* "December Settles in over Haverstraw Bay"; *Dos Passos Review:* "Another Saturday Night"; *The Florida Review:* "Somewhere Over"; *Great River Review:* "Busking"; *Inkwell:* "Sideshow"; *"Innisfree Poetry Journal:* "Crop Duster"; "Nyack, NY: 1/29/02," "When Rachel's Father Moved Away"; *Laurel Review:* "College Town," "Still Life with Signed Iris DeMent Poster, *Infamous Angel* on the Stereo"; *Louisiana Literature:* "Postcard"; *Margie:* "Fish Story"; *McSweeney's:* "Coconut Octopus"; *Ploughshares:* "Buffeted"; *Poetry Southeast:* "Biographical Note"; *The Potomac:* "Tommy's Earthbound Son Gets to Jump Center on Senior Night"; *September 11, 2001: American Writers Respond,* Etruscan Press, 2003: "Crash"; *Tar River Poetry:* "Recipe"; *Virginia Quarterly Review* "Anticipate the Coming Reservoir"

"Fish Story" was reprinted in *Wild, Sweet Notes II: More Great Poetry from West Virginia,* Publishers Place, 2005.
"A Jar of Rain" was reprinted in *Blooming through the Ashes,* Rutgers University Press, 2007.
"Buffeted" was reprinted in *Poetry Calendar,* Alhambra Publishing, 2007.
"Coconut Octopus" was reprinted in *Poetry Calendar,* Alhambra Publishing, 2008.

The publication of this book is made possible by a grant from the Pennsylvania Council on the Arts.

PENNSYLVANIA COUNCIL ON THE ARTS

Library of Congress Control Number 2007931443
ISBN 978-0-88748-480-3
Printed and bound in the United States of America
10   9   8   7   6   5   4   3   2   1

I want to thank Jack Allman, David Baker, Carol and Dick Frost, Bill Heyen, John Martino, Dan Masterson, Toni Morrison, Renee Nicholson, Dave Smith, David St. John, Natasha Trethewey and, especially, Jim Harms and Michael Waters for unflagging friendship and support. I thank as well Jerry Costanzo, Cynthia Lamb, and the Carnegie Mellon University Press staff. I extend my gratitude to Mary Stewart and the *Kestrel* staff, to the New York Foundation for the Arts and the New York State Council on the Arts for a Strategic Opportunity Stipend administered by the Garrison Arts Center in 2006, and to the MacDowell Colony for a Residency Fellowship and a Writer's Aid Grant. "College Town" is for Brenda Boudreau. "Something Is Out There" is for Christy Limbaugh.

For further information, please visit my Web page, which is housed on the *Ploughshares* Web site, www.pshares.org.

CONTENTS

North on the Palisades Parkway

I

II

III

This time for my mother, Maria Hoppenthaler

Puzzled, he walked farther and felt rainy vapor as he leaned almost into darkness. Yes, the stream had already left its banks, and the spreading water was deep enough to dapple like a lake.

—Jayne Anne Phillips

And life went on beyond the Palisades. . . .

—Billy Joel

There was a low fog

and as we drove it parted, and kept
     parting (What else could it do?)
          all the way home.
                    —Stephen Dunn

Around exit two, on my way back
from Manhattan, I enter Hudson fog
so thick & brooding
taillights bloom like bruises, fade,
then disappear to nothing.

The muddy spirits of Lenape & fish rise
from the river, slide up palisades,
& creep through the slit of my open window.
I'm breathing them in—water, ghosts—
Henry Hudson, his crew, Half-Moon
creaking into waves. Seized up
apparitions of gulls spiral down
into a whirling flux of whitecaps.
Long eels slip into my lungs,
curl up there, & sleep.
No boundaries. To follow the curve
of parkway, I rely on sudden
revelations of reflectors, white
stripes seen for an instant,
then lost for seconds on end.
Spectres of shad fishermen,
nets sheared by sweeping headlights,
the whiskered heads of catfish—
ancient sturgeons slowly turn,
& the fog breaks near Orangeburg.
Ghosts drift back to the river. Wings
skitter, dip & flirt; waves shudder,
meander toward the Atlantic,
& I go the other way, home.
Like Henry, I sail hopeful against the current.

I

TREEHOUSE

Take a walk down your block at three
in the morning. Listen to things

obscured by white noise in daytime:
gargle of a gutter at the end

of Limestone Lane; mild groans
from your neighbor's treehouse;

two maples daring just a little
closer to heaven. Vast orchards

of planets spin away into kilter.
Climb the rope ladder hanging there.

Sit in that far corner where high
moons filter through leaves

& over grass clippings, weekend roses
rot on the compost pile. Flickering

bats can barely be glimpsed dipping
darkness. It will be hard to leave

if you do it right. It will be awful
to stand down again on earth.

Frantic icons leapt from a failing desktop,
deep into the cyber abyss & I knew
it was trouble—virus warnings that were

routinely ignored soon flashed
red through my brain. The screen: blank, useless
as keys I kept punching, trying to lock in

& *energize* like wily Scotty on *Star Trek*.
But whir, zap, dispersed & gone to who knows where—
detritus & satellites slapped into

darker regions of the mysterious
universe. Backed up on disks, poetry survives,
though not innocence, risky downloads,

the suspicious, sexy allure of **click here**
lost in space. *Danger, danger.*
And even as earthly tower debris still

smolders, is picked over for clues & miracles,
I'm through being stunned, grateful today
for anger. It will take time till technicians

get the machine online, offer reasons
beyond a simple grasp. With icons restored,
we'll build again toward heaven, hover as we

can between galaxies absurdly distant,
or so close we tend to forget they're here.
Fingers tap buttons, funereal pipers

summon the missing. Tether their smoke
now to lovers born in September. Recover them
like confessions tangled in uncertain histories.

In my dream, I'm clearing bottom
in an upstate county
with a pair of oxen yoked to a plow.
The off ox is sickly
& gaunt. He struggles with his pride
& body to keep up
to the task at hand. In my dream,
my shoulder strains against
the rump of the weaker animal. Stumps
tear free from earth.
In my dream, I start awake to discover
it's my own back end
I'm pushing on, & cold water covers
the village that stood
here once, tragic houses my fathers
built in that wilderness
then had to surrender. In my dream,
my favorite uncle
uncases his fragile fiddle, scrambles
up the mountain's
rocky side to where rattlesnakes
take sun, sense
smoke & spilt blood in the hollow.
For one whole day,
he sparked dew-eyed rattlers while
I picked them off
with a .22 at my leisure, skinned them
clean right then & there.

I was cookin' squirrel meat in the kitchen
when the cold shiver shot up my back.
Outside, a panther crossed the clearin'
near the pens, cryin' awful like a girl.
I could hear whimperin' even after
it disappeared into that stand of laurels
by the water. I knowed there were ghosts
whose lot it was to spook danger spots
along the Delaware; Foul Rift, the worst,
is just beyond the river bend.
I never minded them spirits none, their rafts
smashin' up on the rocks forever and that's
about it for them folk and hereafter.
But this were different. It feeled weird
straight away, and then I knowed what soul
was uneasy out there. When I digged up
ground out back for the barn's foundation,
I upset some bones—Indian bones I figgered.
I plows up their arrowheads all the time,
you know, they was all through these parts.
So I buried them bones best I could
just beyond the trees, said some few words
over them that I knew and believed I was rid
of that. But then I burnt the meat, the damned
panther kept a'keenin' after sheep,
and them shadder rafts torn asunder in the rapids—well,
I been drinkin' a lot too much these days,
but I'm near to give up the stuff for ghosts.
They makes it known that they're troubled,
and they haunts me, you know, they haunts me
till I'm so stinkin' drunk I'll break
into a rowdy verse of "For Heaven's Sake,
McCluskey, Close Yer Valve," a'stompin'
my work boots so loud on the floor they'll
hear it clear down to hell. When my woman died,
I told the damned bees and draped their hives

like I always heard of or she'd'a made off
with their souls, but I'm thinkin' she took off
with mine instead. I keeps a lantern burnin' all night
to scare away the animals. I drifts off to sleep
sounder knowin' there's brightness there,
and don't a jelly jar of applejack shine golden
in that light, like so much honey, my Ellen's blonde hair.
I keep dreamin' of the flood, old graves shoveled up,
them new pine coffins hauled off'n wagons,
and me settin' right here on this damned porch step
with a pocket pint'a white lightnin', a'pointin' out
forgotten landmarks to nobody much at all.

Doesn't the sky press heavily down today?
And doesn't the universe appear to reveal itself
finite and bitter, in the throes of a surly last hurrah?
There are things I might say that are nearly true.
Yes: possibility does have an end, and beginning
here *right here* can only get us to that impasse
more quickly. Or I guess I could suggest it's only
rogue weather's misdirection. Tacky pastel
swatches of horizon in bleary shades of water-
stain and well-thumbed Manila folders. Merely
some few dingy hours before nightfall darkens
to closet us in even further. And how will we
spend proximity? Fill empty folders with what?
You and I both seem to want to be the sky.

RECIPE

I'm the one working the kitchen, making stock
from chicken wing tips I'd saved in the freezer,
some bouillon cubes, the picked-over carcass

of last Sunday's dinner. A gallon of spring water,
celery stalks, a few cloves of garlic for luck &
health, a handful each of sliced carrot & sweet Vidalia
to deepen the color & keep you, dear, rooted

to earth. I'm the one straining out sediment
with a chinois, golden liquid pooling there,
filling the bottom of your mother's favorite bowl,

the one setting broth in the fridge to chill,
scraping off next morning's greasy patina of fat
from the surface—it's been winter here forever!
I'm the one simmering, steaming, ladling soup

over wild rice in your finest kiln-fired crockery,
Chef de Cuisine of intense flavor, of this *oh so
nice* homemade & homely midday decadence.

Oh hearts, leap high!
—they touch in mid-heaven like an acrobat
and make a rainbow
                    —D. H. Lawrence

Two perky women—the sort who'll break
eggs, brew coffee, pant & bear
down—wield their twin strollers in tandem.
They force me off the narrow sidewalk
& into the fast lane where I've never been
at home. From today's Bob Brezsney horoscope:
May you never have a cat-food jingle running
through your head while you're making love. They run—
meow!—& streak through our ordinary sex.
Shame on us for such a smack-dab dire
lack of ingenuity, clumsy choreography.
Do you think it's easy to shave & see
a monster? Villagers aren't kind
& exploit my reasonable fear of fire.
I could change, I swear, but stocks
are reeling. Greenspan's got to adjust
& so do we, so roll the pot & there's
your gold. Leprechauns won't bother
with a fool already chatting up his figments.
The neighbors throw a pig roast,
& hog fat drip drip drips. Darts
at the pub; thud thud thud. Rain
in ashes; mud mud—you
get the picture & look just terrible.
The camera never loved you.
Neither the cat, who hates dry Friskies,
our erect & masterly ways.
One afternoon a deluge slathered
on for twenty minutes, & then
the most perfect rainbow I've ever known
stretched unbroken over the bridge

& river, Westchester side to here.
On the clock radio, rush hour traffic:
forty minute backup on the Rockland bound Tap.
You were late, the cat was scarce,
& I was a monster. The tick tick ticks
measured nearly the length of my dumb,
dark hobbyhorse, exactly the time it took
to conjure up & label—Roy G. Biv—
the whole stained swath of spectrum.

Because they're pretty,
your daughter rips each errant crocus from my lawn.
The cat is wary
under sagging racemes of the laburnum,
& a bedraggled robin drops stupidly from the fence.

I'm wondering who you see
with your eyes tightly shut,
as they're shut now since glare has filtered
through oak branches to highlight your face. Kevin

returns from 7-Eleven with Saranac & Heineken,
vanilla Häagen-Dazs, Fritos & nachos,
a carton of Cheddar Goldfish for Sara. You feign
resignation; you grin & roll those green eyes as she

swoops up fistfuls of Goldfish & teeters off,
trailing crackers carelessly
behind her to blaze in the sun, bright orange crumbs
for squirrels & the birds. Your husband, gone
again to the silver SUV,

comes back clutching just one purchase more,
a simple bouquet of gas station flowers.

More interesting to me were notches and chevrons,
quarter moons snipped free from folded sheets
of construction paper, not the colored "snowflakes"

themselves, taped later to classroom windows
or tacked onto bulletin boards. And bulletin,

indeed, portent of the hardest winter, memorandum
to ominous skies stretching their pall over Clarkstown.
I swept confetti from my desktop and stuffed it

down into corduroy pockets until recess
when I sat alone, crown rung of the monkey bars,

and hurled fistfuls of magic into oak leaves
that swirled, then stalled, then scurried across
the playground blacktop. Small matter,

but still, surly Miss Cruz yelled me down, made me
gather what scraps I could trap under sneakers,

and marched me inside to copy onto loose-leaf
page forty-three of Webster's dictionary. Words
took on their meanings then, arisen from

that schoolboy spell. Winter passed
as well, curling flakes replaced in December

with sloppy cutouts of Christmas trees and menorahs.
More interesting to me, though, were snow angels
lucky fifth graders were spiriting just outside,

jacketed bodies so easily occupying the chilly
spaces their legs and wings had scissored wide.

The temperature holds near seventy; a shirt-sleeved crowd
gathers at Memorial Park to consider the river, toss scraps aloft
to gulls in mid-afternoon. The men of Cool Breeze Mechanical
take a long lunch. No desperation calls for heat today or air,
they munch pizza at their leisure and prepare for summer's arrival.
Local kids are shooting hoops, and every swing is swinging

in the playground as two guitar strummers huddle on a picnic table,
stumble through their skittery repertoires. Even Nickel Joe
stops poking for bottles awhile to grin. I've come to wash away
those days I regret in brackish water. Something awkward
gnaws at the trembling phoenix heart inside my chest. Why ever
blessed in the aftermath, that spiny wreath of last year I'll toss
away as best I can. Black Lab chases Frisbee, comes back, chases

Frisbee, comes back—no end, it seems, to his enthusiasm,
his devotion. And now lovers have come to the quiet gazebo to whisper.
On New Year's Eve I watched fireworks set this skyline ablaze.
I stood outside the bar in blue cold with regulars, cradled delicate
flutes of bubbles in my fingers. We were thinking of towers,
how change had come. Together we wished it meant an early spring.

II

And then there was Bernie Anderson,
who was my lab partner in high school bio.
He hung out with the heavy metal clique,
so when he etched a Manson-inspired cross
into his forehead we didn't think too much about it.
We kept dissecting worms and frogs and fetal pigs.
He passed me a note once asking if huffing
formaldehyde would get us buzzed. That winter,
because he wanted a stigmata bad but
couldn't will himself one, he broke an icicle
from the eave outside his bedroom window,
pounded it clean through his palm with a rubber
hubcap mallet, and sat at his desk while it melted.
Blood and water ran together everywhere.
When they released him from psychiatric care
he was more elusive than ever, hard
to figure but, sure as shit, his right hand showed
the mark and everyone allowed Bernie a certain
eerie credibility. Later that year he killed himself.
Somewhere—maybe it was an urban legend,
or one of those stories he loved by Poe or de Maupassant,
but he bought a trunk full of frozen blocks
from the Nyack Ice Company when his parents
left for three weeks in Spain, tied a rope
to the back rim of his basketball hoop, placed
the noose around his neck as he stood barefoot
on the stack, handcuffed himself behind his back,
then strangled as ice dissolved beneath his toes.
Had it rained or if, as he must have planned it,
he wasn't found until the dark stain dried
on blacktop, it might be mysterious still
how he died with no chair or ladder there,
and I'm sure he wanted that to be a secret.
He'd think his dying a failure. I wouldn't bring
this up now except for the fact that last week
I went to a friend's wedding. The reception
was at a Holiday Inn in Jersey, and I ditched

into the staging area to bum a choke
from a waiter. We smoked out on the loading
dock and there, on a sheet of plastic behind
the dumpster, a chef was hacking out an ice
sculpture of Jesus for the First Christian Church
of the Second World Dinner/Prayer Meeting
with a chain saw, a chisel, and a rubber mallet.
It was warm for late October. Jesus was sweating—
the chef, too, who was cursing and had just
decided to do the fine cosmetic work
in the walk-in freezer or else, he said, "Christ,
Jesus will end up in the storm drain."
"It's a mystery to me," he muttered as he lit
a Lucky Strike, put out the wooden match
with a sizzle on the side of his creation,
"why anyone would want a melting Jesus
in the middle of their savory quiche tarts
and meatballs, but they're paying a freakin' fortune."
Funny how ice dilutes good bourbon just
enough if you drink it with a little urgency.
Let me buy you another;
could I have a cigarette? It's scary
when so much wells up at once.
Got a match? A lighter? Drink up already;
I think our next round is on the tender.

TOMMY'S EARTHBOUND SON GETS TO JUMP CENTER ON SENIOR NIGHT

Cheerleaders flaunting pleated skirts and the off-key high
school jazz band mistreating "Sweet Georgia Brown" are much
more exciting than the game. I make for the lower parking lot,
dark and slightly threatening near the drainage ditch,
snaggle of ragged trees and undergrowth, but it's very quiet,

bright stars embedded in the nine o'clock sky. I think
I'll take a spin through my old stomping grounds, maybe click
into an unencrypted wireless connection with my laptop.
Don't blame me if I Google a trendy poet's Web site, jealously
admire the quality of her links. I'm missing and Tommy's

certain to notice I've vanished. His boy is back on the bench.
The home team's dribbled onto the court; they're taking out the ball.
Second half already and Tommy probably figured I'd hit the can.
By now I'm sure he thinks my suspect heart's petered out, I've keeled
over face first into a urinal. But tonight the pouty cheerleaders

stay beautiful and more than a short hair slutty. When custodians
    reveal
enormous eight-foot dust mops, as Billy Banfield re-counts
concessions stand money, I'll be prying wishing stars free
from their settings—MIA, AWOL, and *Where the fuck?*—
navigating carefully vast nostalgic blocks of Milky Way.

When I return, the half-full trophy case glitters the deserted lobby;
shower heads still drip in the men's locker room; nobody's
left sitting on the bench. With an Allen wrench, someone chocks
the crash bars; metal doors click and lock. Have you ever been
this alone in your alma mater, walking down nearly familiar

hallways in darkness? The feeble glow of an exit sign casts
a blood-washed spotlight on buffed terrazzo. Have you ever acted
out a death scene like mine, soliloquized maybe on this lonely
stage? Have you ever babied and bankrolled a dramatic production
clear through its standing room only, sold out forever, just one
    night run?

The band was mid-space jam, classic segue—
"China Cat Sunflower" into "I Know You Rider,"
Nassau Coliseum a swirl with colored lights.
Danny dripped sweat, dancing frantically before
his seat, black hair flailing his face. Jerking
still a moment, he twitched a few spastic times
as if electrified, then began screaming,
Garcia's Satan; Jerry's the fuckin' devil.
He spun, flew full speed up the aisle, past
startled security guards and out the doors,
shrieking obscenities through the darkness
of eastern Long Island. Half a purple "window
pane" inside me, too, I stayed through encores,
the last bent notes of "Johnny B. Goode," filed
out with Dead Heads as the marijuana smoke,
wafting patchouli billowed into October.
Heading for the Hofstra towers, I slipped beyond
the parking lot and nearly tripped over Danny,
covered in mud, blood seeping from his nose.
He was cowering there, sobbing in the fetal position.
In the dorm room I cleaned him up with dishrags.
He wolfed down Slim Jims with tap water,
collapsed finally onto the stained couch we'd
salvaged together street-side from a pile of junk
and snored away in sighs and fits. I jump-started
my buzz with bong hits, bourbon shooters, cracked
open a tepid Bud and stared as morning began
glazing the campus with light. Twelve years later
Jerry was gone, heart failure while taking the cure
at Serenity Knolls. And Danny Boy? He'd heard
the pipes, the pipes and ended up a hanging judge,
sentenced himself to swing by the neck until
he was dead dead dead. How lucky was I?
Alive enough to turn up loud a bootleg tape
of that show, swirl dusty zinfandel in a fragile glass,

strain to pick out Danny's shouts through dual
drums, noodling guitars, Phil Lesh's thick bass lines.
I want so badly now to know for sure what drove despair,
flash back into that night's tripped-up darkness and help,
forgive at last the devil's sweet riffing, his allure, myself.

Mr. Bones, you a clown
—JB

Dinner tonight is chili dogs with onion, pepperoni rolls,
pitchers of beer at Gene's. Berryman's doppelgänger
slouches at his typical place, far corner of the bar;
once in a while he drowses off into the *terra incognita*
of his beard. For a joke, Brenda reads bumps on my head.
She's been theorizing phrenology for a paper,
& we've been drinking glasses of Rolling Rock
to avoid the ugly stacks of freshman essays we need to grade.
A knot here, a B; a lump there, C. I could shrug & let it go again.
My first week at Clown College I broke out in hives from
                                        greasepaint,
ass backwards discovered claustrophobia in a polka dot VW Bug
crammed with armpits & feet, & those big red noses
chafe & sawdust reeks of elephant piss. That was no place for Bozo.
John's dozed off. Sometimes he ticks like dogs
dreaming what they dream. When he starts awake,
he might be Mr. Bones, or Huffy Henry, or maybe
only John, who needs the john, & creaks right by us on his way.
Who knows what formations give his unkempt scalp geography?
"You must have rocks in your head," Brenda giggles,
& I'd been ready to purr. "In a previous life," I mutter,
"I was stoned to death unjustly. I'm fractured; can't you tell?"
Then John stirs, & Hank, the grinning skeleture of his cat nap.
They light a Camel, & cough, & wheeze, & their single chest
rattles like something hard & loose & probably broken.
Brenda's fingers have disappeared, & the Big Top, too.
Chili dogs woof & bark, grrr in my stomach.
I never learned to walk on stilts. I must have rocks in my head.
John's digging through pockets for a little change, & now
he's having another, just a stone's throw from here.

I was playing love songs on a stolen guitar
when the G string snapped, the few limp
dollars crumpled with change on black fuzz
lining the case. Spring,

Central Park already greening its perennial heart.
I'd be scratching out blues
if there was money in it, but city girls
on the west side want to be honey-

tongued, Motowned, Ah-Angied, Oh Mandyed—
so that's what they get; they get what they want.
Then a cop car wheels by, slowly,
& who could explain the rosewood guitar, the dangling wire?

East side girls want to be Oh Girled, Brown Eyed Girled,
Beach Boyed till dawn,
& summer sun bleaches my hair so blonde
even the suburbs seem possible.

There are girls who'll linger in Nyack, flirt
through Ossining, & I can act, & I can sing.

O. marginatus

Hydrostatic pressure defines the pulsing shape
of an octopus. *marginatus* dwells among sunken
coconuts, more than fifty feet deep, hiding
sometimes in its shell by drawing two halves around
its body. When faced with danger, it wraps six arms
around itself and backpedals away on a pair, camouflaged,

innocent coconut bob bobbing along. Camouflaged,
eluding predators with admirable stealth—shape-
shifter—the suckered treads of its fluid-filled arms
rolling slowly over ocean bottom, past sunken
shipwrecks, intrusive snorklers who dive around
the coastline of Indonesia. What glorious hiding,

so utterly naked and in open sight! Such stealthy hiding
can excite though, really, the ingenious camouflage
of *marginatus* is stereotyped, an inherent moving around
requiring no feedback from the brain. The shape,
color, not more than oblivious twitching of nerves, sunken
coconuts a coincidence of seascape to which it adjusts. Armed

only with behavior coded into the ganglia of each arm,
it could care less about any potential thrill of its hiding.
Ignorance and bliss. I'm looking hard at my face: sunken
blue eyes, tidal drift of hairline, the graying camouflage
of a beard. My fantasies are all about being in better shape,
spaced-out moments spent realizing that I've been around

a pretty long time. Each creature in the food chain is surrounded
by gourmands and midnight snackers, swollen armies
of gluttonous neighbors whose grotesque shapes
mirror the intensity of their desire. Here I am hiding
out in the flotsam of suburbia. I'm camouflaged
as pocket lint, later as a soul who knows how low to sink,

how thrilling to buoy among wind-fallen coconuts. At the
　　kitchen sink,
I'm preparing octopus while a lover seems still around
to enjoy it; she's curled up on the sofa, camouflaged:
comfy bolster, shadow. I could hold her in my arms.
Remove ink sac, eyes, and teeth. Clean well. "Oh, hide

from me, will you?" *Place in a pot; simmer till tender.* "Oh, shapely,
shapely. Oh, sunken treasure; seductress." *Cut the eight arms
into bite-sized pieces.* Around every corner, she's hiding there.
In coconut cream, camouflaged, roiling, assuming another shape.

Stoned in the canned jangle of steel
drum tunes in the faux Tiki bar, I sit below
dusty plastic fronds and nurse my drink. A few stools
down, too precious for words, a tongue-studded, nose-ringed,
lesbian couple, heads bowed close, whisper secrets and softly laugh.
I want their love to last.

I order a plate of clams oreganato
with crusty French bread on the side for dipping
into the buttery broth that strongly hints at salty brine.
Ted slides another frozen margarita down the lacquered
surface of the bar top while some raw, tequilaed-up synapse fires,
and I remember the Paul Simon

song that mentions two fragile ex-lovers
speculating over who's been damaged the most.
Guess what?: I think of you: how much like the book
you said you could read me like this is of me: to flounder
still in our marred way of being together in the world. I love the dead,
dumb clack of emptied shells

as I assemble them into a stylized pile, as if
building an already weathered monument to sailors
the night sea took away and never gave back. Damaged
dreamboat. Damaged land. Damaged ocean. Damaged man.
Damaged woman. Damaged tide. Damaged moon. Damaged pride
Damaged angel. Damaged wing.

Damaged Jesus. Damaged everything. I don't think
it will last, though the adorable lovers have now gathered
tightly in each other's arms and seem, in this heartbeat, defiantly
inextricable, their matching dragonfly tattoos now visible, poised as if
for trans-Atlantic flight on each girl's right shoulder blade. I think
of the artist's needle, how it broke the skin.

Empty, even the wine bottle
surrenders the ocean's desire.

You take the conch from my hand
& slowly raise it to your ear,

put fingers to my nipples;
a trickle of water wanders

down my chest. A whisper.
Whatever was said lost

in the meander of waves,
possible whorls of language.

You pick tiny slivers of shell
from my back & hold them in your palm—

tidal jewels. Listen:
each mermaid mouths

her name to the breakers.
Your tongue traces moisture

down the curve of my body; licking
waves welcome & offer. Shy

as young lovers, they touch, stir
the sand, & return each time.

& so this beach, for all its sunshine
& the ripe smell of banana tanning oil
drifting toward me from Erin's blanket,
seems almost wrong,
the fact I know her only by name, loosed to seagulls
by a best friend. Or maybe she's the close stepsister
from her mother's second marriage that just didn't take. . . .

& there's the old woman with a paper bag,
snatching up perfect shells
(her hair was once as red as embers)
to sell to the gift shop on A1A.
Erin's hair is blonde, sun-flecked, feathered
back like undertow. I am not dreaming, I. . . .

She glistens. The slick sheen of her
is more than I can bear, the gleaming coil of her snake tattoo—
these waves, they reach out for you, or
Erin, who's walked to the water,
& if you were here I'd tell you just that.

It's a pretty long road trip to *wherever*
and so, tired finally of singalongs,

shouting out tags from exotic states,
we strip off one piece of clothing each exit,

saving for last the modesty of safety belts. Free
as we are, I pull off and we fuck

behind the risky cover of a Dairy Queen.
Tomorrow we may well slip

into an idle Hyatt coatroom, thrash
against the racks awhile,

newborn reptiles ripping their leathery shells,
hangers clattering brassy music.

Just last week, in the mathematics building,
the elevator lurched; you yanked

your pointy teeth away,
and when the door slid open hid

with your body my obvious affection.
The elderly professor who'd summoned

our disarray seemed hardly to notice;
a nod of his gray head appeared a blessing.

Mere predictability, he might offer,
is a fool's game and it can only go so far.

> *Silver wings shining in the sunlight. . . .*
> —Merle Haggard

Tonight I am a sucker
for every sad song on the radio.
I've requested them for hours,
back & forth between stations,
adjusting to static,
disguising my voice to deejays.
Play me that tune by the Chi-Lites, no, Nilsson,
"I Can't Live (If Living Is Without You)."
On the nearly full 747, flying
home from Florida tanned but alone,
I touched the long hair of the woman
sitting before me. It was beautiful
hair, auburn, cascading there
down the small of her back like rainfall—
I touched it because I needed to.
The second time because I wanted to,
the last for luck, hers & mine, & yours, too—
I can be a graceful loser if not a good one.
Play Otis, "You Don't Miss Your Water,"
Patsy Cline, "Three Cigarettes In An Ashtray."
On the plane, specifics predictably wrong,
it was Merle Haggard I sang to myself
through the baffled syntax of turbulence—
Don't take that airplane ride. Her hair—
ride her hair; it's what I wanted to do:
magic carpet, Rapunzel.
There's time before careless morning
shows jar the airwaves for Procol Harum,
"Love Hurts"—or Kristofferson—
"Take the ribbon from your hair.
Shake it loose & let it fall."

By the time
        ("I get to Phoenix")
I staggered into the terminal
        ("She'll be rising")
she was gone from sight,
        silver wings.

III

I'm hunched over a slice at Totonno's.
I've come to keep from forgetting.
You get sand in your shoes, you never can leave.

Carnies bury their dead under the Wonder Wheel.
Mermaid Queen, Bambi, says it beats the Cyclone for petting.
Grease drips from a slice at Totonno's.

What developer's freak show does Neptune conceal?
Everything closed. It was all very slum. It started coming....
You get sand in your shoes, you never can leave.

Six hundred pound Lola wed three-foot Prince Hal.
I consider Horse-Faced Milo, galloping, galloping,
sprinkle red pepper flakes on a slice at Totonno's.

Hannah the Bear Girl—I remember her smile.
Bambi walks *in the footsteps*, the old *glamour, fading.*
You get sand in your shoes, you never can leave.

The big ticket today is minor league baseball.
You didn't go out of Coney Island for anything.
I'm hunched over a slice at Totonno's.
You get sand in your shoes, you never can leave.

You tie off the stringer to a root, let three
brookies drift in a pool. When you return
from a few casts downstream, dozens of crayfish
are shredding your trout to pieces. Bombarding
them with big rocks **feels** good, but there goes dinner.
You think: *étouffée!* but any crawdads
still able have quickly scuttled away.
You remind yourself: *I'm here to relax,*
decide on chicken fried steak & mashed
at Stan's Greedy Spoon. Since you can, you flirt
with the waitress, order a pitcher of Budweiser—
two glasses—& scan the local paper.
Because she's curious—you'd been certain she'd ask—
you lie again & tell her stories. What the hell
else to do anyway before nightfall, then
a final trip to the bait shack your last morning here?
You say the extra glass is for Joey,
lost in the Gulf. Or Eddie, crushed flat
by falling trees. Or Kelly, sweet Kelly,
who keeps dying in your miserable heart.
She's wearing the tell-tale tie-dyed tee-shirt,
so you blurt out it's for Jerry Garcia, too,
& she sits & you both light cigarettes.
The carnival's in town, "it's been real slow,"
& you're both laughing & getting friendly
when a trooper pops in for a pizza burger to go.
Like every other stoner who did drugs
in the seventies, who'll still fire up a fat one
every now & then, cops make you nervous, their
studied dead fish demeanor. But he smiles
at you, winks at Clara who seems familiar,
& says he's so hungry he'll have cherry pie
with supper, "just wrap it up." He lights
a smoke himself. So there we are awhile.
He says last night he nearly busted dwarves
for their drunken joyride down High Street

but drove them instead to trailer town,
"two tipsy midgets &, get this," he says,
"Cherry Bomb, the human cannonball.
The one driving, what a spectacle:
him walking the line, touching every part
of his face but his nose, but how could I
arrest them & ever hear the end of it
at the barracks? Besides," he says, "it can't be easy,
their runty, little lives." He takes up the sack,
wishes me good fishing, shakes his crew cut,
& tells Clara he'll stop by tomorrow. She grins
when he leaves, slides two coins into the juke box,
presses buttons for "Scarlet Begonias,"
& warbles along, dancing back to my table.
"She had rings on her fingers & bells on her shoes,
& I could tell without asking she was into the blues.
I love the Dead," she admits, "but you
had that figured. Spin another story. Tell me
something I don't already know. He won't be back,
not Stanley either. It's me. All me." & she pours
out lager into an empty glass as if she owned it.

The whorl of a slim thumbprint—
your hand had grasped the glass so tightly.
Inhaling at the rim, still
Scotch whisky smoke
as on our lips last night, slurred
kisses. Remember the hollow shake
of ice cubes, sorry
wads of tissue paper tossed
away onto the rickety coffee table?
Sillier yet how we celebrated
goodbye, chicken wings—heat lamp dry—
at Kentucky Fried, then exploring together
the seven aisles of a grocery store
in an unfamiliar part of town. We found
cranberry ginger ale, Cajun specialties,
dewy bunches of cilantro cheap as lettuce,
sailed a gray-tiled way through *terra
incognita*. We left tentative prints
on jars of mango chutney and low-fat dip.
Tropical fingers brushed my face.

At the high school reunion our singleness
draws us finally together. I say nothing
has ever worked out. Years of grad school,

predictable struggles later. Soon I blame it
on suburbia, everyone married there with kids

and the rest too young or desperate or off
their medication. She dishes: *Divorce. Career.*
Mistakes. Our clichéd blah blah blahing

is more sad than awkward. Wagging tongues
grow prominent and fat; the chosen words

are maudlin foreplay. We end up at last doing
the eye thing: mine, she says, are *blue* and *cool,*
like those of every plastic dolly she'd ever clutched

as a girl. And yours, I snicker, are milk chocolate-
brown and seem as though they'd melt for sure

left carelessly on a summer dashboard.
The quick scowl on her face—I figure it
a character flaw suddenly revealed, dread

of Happy Hour consolations I've been living by.
And now it's time for dessert. *That thick slab of pie*

looks so fucking yummy, she sighs.
Whipped cream.
Cherry.

a week ago, she began to sing and still
hasn't stopped. I hear her now,
trilling through leaves, perched high
in the farthest crook of the apple tree.
Her mother's concerned. "Rachel
doesn't sing well," she jokes, forcing
a grin. "It's hard hearing her lullabies
falling asleep at night, and what
about school? Maybe it's just a phase."
Walking over to the gnarled trunk,
she grabs hold of each end of a board
he'd nailed there to serve as a ladder,
peers through the branches. "Rach',
sweetie, how about a sandwich?"
But Rachel isn't hungry. Suddenly
much younger, she's into a sing-a-long
learned years ago from Barney,
that lavender dinosaur on TV:
"I love you, you love me," she chants, picks
a big, green apple. She takes a bite
and it's bitter; then, she takes another.

Afternoons they often wandered through malls,
and he held in his hands small objects of growing
        desire. One time a purple Duncan Yo-Yo,
        then a plastic revolver that spat diaphanous

        streams of tap water. Today he might have chosen
        the yellow Tonka dump truck or screaming red
fire engine, but instead he picked out the crop duster
because battery-powered propellers spun at the flick

of his finger. For months now, wanting to keep him
in a safer place than home, his grandmother has taken
        the child away each time her only son's anger scorched
        the thin fabric of his marriage—always it seemed just

        as it had been ironed again to threadbare smoothness.
        She sips a cherry Coke while he sprawls over
simple patterns sewn into her old Persian rug.
When has it been easier to love one's own

hidden scars? The boy grown bored, tired
flaying back room air with his toy, begins
        to complain, says the plane just goes and goes
        but never takes off. He wants to see it fly.

STILL LIFE WITH SIGNED IRIS DEMENT POSTER, *INFAMOUS ANGEL* ON THE STEREO

My heart
feels like it's burning, though maybe it's just
microwave fallout, radiant heat
of coronary stents so recently
lodged inside an artery. Pierogi
I've doctored with white pepper and onion
have taken on new meaning now that I'm
in love with you, or suffering gastric
indignity, or—antacid aside—
am I having another heart attack?
Sure I'm trying to be cute, turning nights
spent sorry for myself into a joke.
It's how I handle most things. My heart burns
as if it were shoveled full of desert,
as if a bottle of Courvoisier's
been poured straight into my left atrium,
as if you've finally dropped the lit match
onto my lighter-fluid soaked pump house.
Don't look
so innocent. The fire's suspicious
and you're the suspected accelerant.
All that aside, and seriously now,
my heart's burning and every passing
week it gets worse. Were I worried less
about bad luck, I'd revel in apples
hissing and spitting away on coals, just where
they landed when *you tipped my apple cart;*
now it's hotter than Mojave in
my heart.

Imagine party balloons tied
to a fence post one minute,
untethered the next,
Mylar glinting like spacecraft,
curiosity filling
the infinite & entire sky.

What if you reached into your pocket
& found the slip of paper on which
I'd written my important delusions
and the one thing I was sure I knew?
How would you guess it got there?

(You didn't feel my hand?) Truth is,
I didn't know the scrap was gone,
& I've forgotten what I'd scrawled,
but could we finally gather together
with laughter in the dusty sprawl of leaves?

A FALL POEM

On this morning walk
I feel my tendons pull,

release, arms swinging,
tense, blood-red leaves

in the clammy sweep of air.
Sluggish grasshoppers. Tattered

webs draped from branches.
The silent snap at the stem,

twisting drop, leaves
scattered beneath the dogwood.

Soon a tee-shirt won't suffice,
icy skins on puddles

melting into fragile sunlight.
But then the stiff, electric

twitch of a gray squirrel's tail
who picks his way up the trunk

of one blue spruce—soon
the rising wood smoke, soon

joyous raking,
old blankets full of wine-red leaves.

Wrapped in threadbare & faded
cotton towels, snuggled
between the hub & Beth Ann's
sneakered feet, the faint
sloshing of jarred rainwater
too muffled to hear
above road whine & Rolling
Stones on the tape deck.
But like some rare & fragile
egg, she nestled it
there all four hundred long miles
east to Manhattan.
When her brother left Wheeling,
it had been springtime.
He allowed how he'd miss it—
yearning green mountains,
misty Ohio River,
& mostly the rain,
how it sluiced off mom's rooftop
to collect & brim
in an old metal oil drum,
how when he would thwack
its steel side with his finger,
rings would shiver toward
dark water's chilly center.
He would miss the rain,
& they would miss him,
gone to the city, dream job
among skyscrapers
the "big break" of his young life.
They'd sung the theme from
The Mary Tyler Moore Show
together that night
he first heard he'd been hired
& flung cloth napkins
high at the kitchen ceiling,

"You're gonna make it
after all" deflecting off
walls & rising like
hymnal passages till dawn.
Alvin hit a bump.
Careful, she hissed, her left leg
swiveling on raised
toes, hard up against the jar.
It was what she could
still do, the only thing more:
to wash what ashes
were left of his—gutter
to river to sea—
with West Virginia rainfall
dipped up from a drum
whose surface October had
started to freeze over.
Mick Jagger was belting out
"Paint It Black." She saw
the brimming hole in a sky-
line she'd never seen
before begin to unfold.

The first heart attack took away
my fear of dying. I was thirty,
and then my father's third took him.

He blamed himself for my affliction—
genetics—but I had a hand and silver spoon
in it, enough booze to dazzle and daze,

render numb even what was good.
My second MI made off with youth
when I was thirty-nine. Last year hurricanes

swept beaches from the Space Coast
of Florida, even the stretch a block
from my mother's condo. The stroke

tried its best to whisk her away,
succeeded only partially though it had
its way with me, enough booze

to smother more than I care to remember.
And the dazzling green parrot I found
splayed curbside while power walking—

at first I swore it was a stuffed animal,
some child's faux conure fallen from a stroller,
but it was real, passed on. It was—I know, I'm sorry—

an **ex**-parrot, and even that quick, black
flash of Monty Python shtick hardly let me
crack a grin, barely caused me to blubber at all

once I settled on an Early Bird dinner
with the house Chianti. God, I'm forty-four.
Float in a sand barge; replace the beach.

Nail the parrot's stiff corpse to a wooden perch.
Let the fake one up and soar, dazzle and daze.
It's nobody's fault. Take it away. Take it away.

"North on the Palisade's Parkway": Epigraph is from Stephen Dunn's poem, "The Dinner."

"Ashokan: A Catskill Story": In the early to mid 1900s, a number of small upstate towns and villages in New York's Esopus Valley were condemned under the law of eminent domain and flooded to create a reservoir system that now supplies New York City with billions of gallons of water. This poem, as does "Anticipate the Coming Reservoir," owes a debt to *I Walked the Road Again: Great Stories from the Catskill Mountains,* edited by Janis Benincasa and published by Purple Mountain Press in 1994. I particularly wish to acknowledge those chapters written by Norman Studer.

"Somewhere Over": Bob Brezsney writes a popular syndicated horoscope. The acronym Roy G. Biv is a popular mnemonic device used for memorizing the colors of the spectrum and their traditional order.

"Buffeted": Refers to the Paul Simon song, "Hearts & Bones."

"Sideshow": This sloppy villanelle owes a great debt to Chris Erikson's 6/24/06 *New York Post* article on Coney Island. Occasionally altered, italicized passages reflect the words of those residents he interviewed. Totonno's is a landmark pizza parlor on Neptune Avenue. Keyspan Park is the home of the Brooklyn Cyclones, a New York Mets minor league affiliate.

"Still Life with Signed Iris DeMent Poster, *Infamous Angel* on the Stereo": Refers to the song "Hotter Than Mojave in My Heart." *Infamous Angel* is available from Warner Brothers Records.

2006
Burn the Field, Amy Beeder
Dog Star Delicatessen: New and Selected Poems 1979–2006,
    Mekeel McBride
The Sadness of Others, Hayan Charara
A Grammar to Waking, Nancy Eimers
Shinemaster, Michael McFee
Eastern Mountain Time, Joyce Peseroff
Dragging the Lake, Robert Thomas

2007
So I Will Till the Ground, Gregory Djanikian
Trick Pear, Suzanne Cleary
Indeed I Was Pleased With the World, Mary Ruefle
The Situation, John Skoyles
One Season Behind, Sarah Rosenblatt
The Playhouse Near Dark, Elizabeth Holmes
Drift and Pulse, Kathleen Halme
Black Threads, Jeff Friedman
On the Vanishing of Large Creatures, Susan Hutton

2008
The Grace of Necessity, Samuel Green
After West, James Harms
The Book of Sleep, Eleanor Stanford
Anticipate the Coming Reservoir, John Hoppenthaler
Parable Hunter, Ricardo Pau-Llosa
Convertible Night, Flurry of Stones, Dzvinia Orlowsky